PLANNING AS A MANAGEMENT TOOL FOR ACHIEVING ORGANIZATIONAL EFFICIENCY

BY

APEIYE GOODLUCK.

Copyright © 2018 apeiyegoodluck

apeiyegoodluck@gmail.com

+2348131971364

First Edition 2018

ISBN:978-1717138514
ISBN-13:978-1717138514

DEDICATION

This book is dedicated to the almighty God the source of my inspiration. To my sweetheart, MRS IDRIS HAWA Hope who believe greatly in me and always eager to invest in me. Dearly, your type is rear. I love you.

To my sweet mother, MRS. GRACE APEIYE who greatly believes in what I will become and always want to do everything to make me happy and comfortable wherever I am, Mum, you are the best.

To all business operators who lacks the power to make alternative course of action, as those who doesn't know how to plan in business, I want to say don't let your business go liquidating or bankrupt; don't give up in your business. The sky is your limit. Am seeing you at the top of your business career!

CONTENTS

DEDICATION

ACKNOWLEDGEMENT

FOREWARD

INTRODUCTION

CHAPTERS

ACKNOWLEDGEMENT

My special gratitude goes to my father, my creator and my general overseer, the creator of the whole universe. Thank you for your guidance in the course of writing from the starting point of this book to its end point

FOREWARD

My Mum a bornafide Christian calls me God never sleeps. Infect she regards me as the one son who reassembles her in characters so much and loved me like the way she loves the rest of her children. She is a delight to me. Our neighbors complain all day that their business doesn't flourish at all even my dad sometime complain about our agro business.

I became sick and tired of these complains and became curious to study business. My dad sees in me the hunger and thirst to become a great business manager.

A day came when he walked

up to me, and inspired me as a graduate I should take over our agro business because I have studied business management I was persuaded by his words and as I took over the business, gradually, we started experiencing positive changes turnover and better results.

In the dream I hard, I saw business dying, managers, administrators, directors complaining and getting discouraged in their business careers and when I woke up I felt bad. I understood everything in life must come from a plan.

No business can do without planning. When a manager lacks the power or ability to plan for the future of his business, he shall experience failure or stagnancy. or This pushed me into writing to help upcoming business tycoons, managers, investors, directors, administrators etc, build their business careers through planning.

INTRODUCTION. TO PLANNING

PLANNING is a process of determining an organization objectives as well as selecting a future cause of action to accomplish such objective.

It means deceiving the present what to do in future. It can also be viewed as the process of recording company's resources in the future with its objective and opportunities.

CHAPTERS

CHAPTER 1

PLANNING

PLANNING as the name implies is defined as the act of setting good and devising specific procedures and schedules for meeting the goals or objectives. It entails the determination of organizational objectives and strategies to be applied to achieve the goals.

It is a manager decision making functions that require the ability to make an alternative course of action. Planning is inevitable in any organization large or small most especially when economic and other Market Condition in the business environment raise challenges to the business.

Planning may be done formerly or informally in simple and sophisticated manner.

most business organizations in the world today, has been running into serious losses to the extent of going bankrupt. This is due to poor planning for the business organization resources.

The failure of some managers to recognize the variety of plan has often caused difficulty in making planning effective.

Its therefore the function of managers and administrators etc. to carry out research and highlight the need for proper planning, identify the basic planning tools and how they can best be applied in modern day system.

Planning is crucial to management because it begins with the determination of an organization objective and designing strategies and technical programmes to achieve these objectives which collate into corporate objective of any organization.

Some firm plan but apply it poorly. This is not encouraging at all. Any good manager is required to plan ahead so that the business will not collapse or liquidate.

CHAPTER 2

MANAGEMENT PLANNING

The primary objective of any business is profit making. If there is no proper planning, the organization may end up not achieving its objective, so there is need for proper planning especially in organizations that engages in manufacturing and marketing of service. It is a manager decision making function that requires the ability to select form alternative course at action.

Planning also requires the preparation at a schedule that anticipate when various goals will be met
. The manager should be imitative enough by developing new ideas in search for better ways of arraying out every function of the organization. Through planning, the management is able to stimulate event and their possible repercussion before they actually occur.

This help in avoiding costly mistake mapping out plan allow its assessment and revision where necessary to achieve a more acceptable result.
 Planning narrow the possible renege of choice thereby making the task of decision making more manageable and less time consuming.

CHAPTER 3

TYPES OF PLANNING

There are two levels of planning. They are

(1) Operational level of planning and

(2) The executive level of planning.

OPERATIONAL LEVEL OF PLANNING

The operational planning is a subset of strategic work planning. It describes short term ways of achieving undertone. It explains how the organization plan to carry out his day to day activities in keeping the firm going to meet its goals.

THE EXECUTIVE LEVEL OF PLANNING

This on the other hand is limited to separate department or functional cities. It is narrowing scope, short range are more concrete. It is lower planning because it relied considerably on prior planning decision of the executive cadre in the organization.

Essentially, planning is a hierarchical activity with a natural sequence and flow of planning decision from the highest to the lowest level of the organization from the executive level of operation to the operational level of organization.

All business men and women to some extent engage in planning but don't give adequate attention to executive level of planning. Thus this altitude is most prevalent among small business owners.

This could be attributed to the fact that most small scale business is started by technical entrepreneurs who by their nature practice oriented and as such are not patient enough to go through the ragouts of broad concept and abstract ideas.

Another reason is by the nature of small business, the chief executive is able to carry out several functions at various level in the organization, since he is deeply involved in the daily operational problem of the business, he overlooks the seemingly more remote higher order planning responsibilities. The small business owner simply assumes that, it's a waste of time to formally state enterprise objective which are self evident.

The first responsibility from top management is to develop a master plan which is the basic successful operation of any business. The master plan guide the small businessman in knowing what he want by setting his enterprise objectives, policies programmes and procedures for achieving and impersonal economy.

CHAPTER 4

THE ESSENCE OF PLANNING

Planning can be called an anticipative decision making

process, where one determines a predicted arrangement of conditions, aims and measures of action in future with acknowledgement of the features of the system in relation to which the actions have been planned. The main focus in planning is finding an answer to the question of how the organization is going to achieve the determined goals.

Planning can be two folds. One approach where one needs to describe the reality from the point of view of the present within available resources and the circumstances under which a vision of the future will be determined.

The second approach is more creative and practical. It is about imagining the future according to our expectations and an attempt to adjust the present reality to the imagined state. It is the realization of vision. In the first and second approach.. The created vision of future allows planning control in relation to the whole organization.

In relation, the essence of master planning in the which sets the tactical and operational strategic plans, the management process starts from where the goals, programmes or strategies are planned which are expected to be implemented in the context of possible use of tangible and intangible resource. It is related to both preparation and constant making of worked out decisions.

Thus strategic planning in management can still be identified as systematic effort to produce basic decisions and actions, which creates and manage the organization. At the same time, they Answer the questions of both whom it is (the organization) and why it does what it does..

At the beginning of the process, we need to set the boundaries of strategic planning by determining the scope of methods and techniques to be used. Next, you need to assume that some of the need of strategic planning will naturally change in time, which may cause the necessity to fill in the planning gap and competition strategy gap by ad-hoc or system decisions to strengthen the state ability to compete as a whole.

CHAPTER 5

DECISIONS AND THEIR CLASSIFICATION

Making decisions is a constant and integral process of choosing such solution that would be seen as effective. From the point of view of management sciences, in decision making, two basic approaches can be distinguished.

First, Normative or Predescriptive determining constant and universal action schemes, and second is the Descriptive, involving the reproduction of processes or activities carried out in a specific reality.
At the same decision making models in general understanding may be quantified. As rational (normative approach) or intuitive (descriptive approach), and their combination and interpenetration can build new models

However, in practice of decision making, the decision maker rarely uses fully rational decision making models since problems are usually not only complex but also difficult to quantify. Derived from classical economy, rationality of expectations in the context of a model business entity, homo economics is detached from reality.

Decisions or decision making expectations can only be reasonable and not rational and cognitive limitations.
Therefore, the models of so called bounded rationality of decision making were developed: heuristic behavior called dual process with a clear line of demarcation combining decisive intuition and rational analysis e.g. within cognitive continuum Theory.

It seems that the approaches combining in parallel rationality and intuition within skills and abilities focused on conscious and unconscious thinking and conclusions are often us in managerial practice.

In business management, decision maker must learn to accept chaos existing in modern global economy. This means that the decisions made today and appropriate from today's perspective, may change tomorrow whether good or bad.

Decision making in conditions of certainty, Risk and Uncertainty in a modern world producing surplus of information and at the same time, information deficits, making personal decision, especially institutional ones becomes exceptionally complicated and demanding.

It is the fact that even the best and the most efficient Intellect of a given decision maker can be highly insufficient.

It is necessary to use the array of decision making instruments which draw on such sciences as psychology, sociology, political science, economics, law and others. On the one hand, it is about diagnosing and pointing out how a given fragment of reality works, while it's descriptive and normative definition.

The subject making a decision can make it only when he is able to determine a set of variations from which he will choose another variant decision. The so called set of permissible variants including awareness of circumstances and Conditions restricting it.

The person had the ability to differentiate among the variants and freedom to choose the one he decided on.

At the same time it has been proven that managers familiar with making strategic decisions asked for it to spend small amount of energy for brain work in opposition to inexperienced people, who perceived the problem of strategic choices as difficult, and their brain needs much more energy to initiate work.

On the other hand, the decision maker has less and less possibilities of making a decision in conditions of certainty, thus it is deterministic.
The undertaken action simply does not have to lead to a specified and planned result.
On the other hand it is difficult to make clearly evaluative and normative judgments within optimal choice, even with the use of dedicated operational and systematic research.

As a result, when it is known, which decision to make, the decision making issues occur in terms of costs, grains, loses opportunities or threats related to that choice.
Probabilistic decisions that are made in conditions of risk are characterized with high uncertainty.
It is, however, possible to estimate the probability of occurrence of specific events.
This facilitates making the right decision, however does not guarantee certainty of such approach.
In this system, decision should be made by the principle of expected utility rather than the Principle of expected value.

When decisions are made in Conditions of complete or partial uncertainty, we can talk about the unpredictability of considered activities.
Decisions made in this regard are discussed in a broad context of game theory if they relate to any opponent.

CHAPTER 6

HETEROGENEOUS KNOWLEDGE IN STRATEGIC PLANNING AND DECISION MAKING

Implementing strategic plans at all levels of state institutions is usually threatened with bigger or smaller failures in some areas.

The difficulties appear not only in realizing goals oriented at certain results, but also in adjusting the annual activity plans to state strategic plans and long term goals in the given scope.

Responsible for it are very often. Only managers of public organizations, who simply do not work, like managers of private organizations, the reason is the lack of adequate resource, in particular of financial character.

It means, that public organizations and their managers should today starts to look for new, more creative ways to draw conclusions from occurring trends, make a realistic evaluation of own possibilities of action and clearly determine which situations and event may evade the counteraction or reacting possibilities.

An open question for individual response remains how the future manager of public sector expresses acceptance to endorse a given institution or government and how is faced with the necessity to choose between the current position and inability to manage, and resigning from the current function in the name of Principles and individual ideals, which entails losing the position and remuneration he is entitled to.

The decisions arrived at must be actual instead of only declaratively, make public values real, like e.g. responsibility, transparency , ability to act quality. They need to consider the fact that public service should entail constant employment of external counselors to solve a given problem or realize a given project within planned actions.

However, one should exceptionally carefully decide, which services can be developed within public and private partnership or privatization or so far public activities. Taking into consideration not only the financial results, but also common good and satisfaction of guaranteed needs.
Determining the developmental needs of an organization, the state is required to conduct strategic analyses, which will set grounds for decision making.

 In this matter, the key meaning have time, dynamics of communication and information exchange. From the point of view, of decision makers, it is very important, whether such dynamics leads to capturing the information from heterogeneous sources and their effective aggregation.

DECISION MAKING IN BUSINESS

DECISION

Is the making of choice among alternative cause of action. No business can operate without making a decision   since all business action are the consequences of some management decision. Decision arrived at today were influenced by those made in the past and in turn, they will affect future decisions. Any decision made by business. Decision are commitment made today for a better tomorrow.

CHAPTER 7

THE NEED FOR PLANNING

The following are the needs for planning, these includes:

(1) Minimize Risk: Risk is often defined as the standard deviation of the return on total investment degree of uncertainty of return on asset. Therefore planning can help to minimize devotion because individual or unit operations through planning know what is expected to be achieved in the organization.

(2) Identification of new technology: since planning process entails mostly storing and finding out workable and. better means of achieving result, New ideas are given birth to by planning on how best to do things in a better cheapest and fastest result hence aiming at new technology.

(3) Give direction: Good planning Give birth to having the sense of direction. In all units or section of the organization.

That is to say, the organization should be directed towards one management goal.

(4) Provide for efficiency: if individuals are good in their different field by doing what is expected or apportioned to them effectively without wasting time, money or energy.

(5) Provision for standard: planning help to arrive at an accepted way often.

This could be in terms of production Marketing requirement to retirement.

(6) Unity of purpose: This lay emphasis on the fact that no individual worker at any level has his own objective. The whole organization is driven by one unit plan.

CLASSIFICATION OF PLAN

Planning could be classified into the following

(1) Strategic Action plan: The top executive are normally responsible for developing strategic action plans which are based on macro approaches for anglicizing organizational features, resources and the environment.

(2) Tactical Action Plan: They are development at the division or department level, which are specified activities that must be performed, which must be completed and what resources a division or department will need to cap the portions of strategic action cover in a period of one or two years.

(3) Operational action plan: They are plans that are normally created by line managers and employees who are directly responsible for carrying out certain tasks or activities. These plans tend to narrowly focused on resources method, timeline

and quality control issues for particular kind of operation.

CHAPTER 9

TIME FRAME FOR PLANNING

A time frame for planning varies widely on organization mission and goals. Each level of management in an organization has their plan and depends on the corresponding time frames. There are three types of time frame planning namely

(1) Long range plans

(2) Intermediate plan

(3) Short range plan

(1) Long range plans: The long range plan is required by top management to make strategic plans in the organization. It covers many years as from five years and over. Whoever, most managers recognized and consider the dynamite environment of the organization when making plans.

(2) Intermediate plans: This type of plan is required by the managers for tactical planning in the organization. It covers a period between one year to five years. This plan is easily subject to change than long range plan.

The intermediate planning is a central focus of planning activities for much organization because it helps to control and monitor the operation of the organization respond to environmental change.

(3) Short range plan: This is the type of time frame required by low or lower or operational management manager to make operational plan s, this type of plan covers a maximum period of one year and it is needed to control the day to day activities of the organization.

Advantages of Planning

(1) It helps to identify unforeseen pitiful

(2) It serves as eye to identify opportunities

(3) It helps to systematically forecast the future

(4) It set standards that spends control

(5) It enhance efficiency

(6) It provides for better coordination, hence achieving standardization.

Disadvantages of Planning

Despite the numerous advantages of planning, there are some limitations the uses of planning.

Planning is limited by the accuracy of information and future fact.

(1) Planning is costly

(2). planning still initiative

(3). Planning delays actions

(4) Planning is overdone by planners

(5).planning has limited practical value.

SUMMARY

Planning is the act of determining an organization objectives as well as selecting   a future cause of action to accomplish such objectives.

 There are two types of planning, operational and the executive. The need why management should plan is to minimize risk, identify new technology, via directives, and provide for refinancing.

Findings

The steps of planning consist of the following. These include:

a. Being aware of opportunities

b. Establishing objectives

c. Developing primaries

d. Determining alternative cause of action

e. Evaluating alternative cause

f. Selecting a cause

g. Formulating derivative plans

h. Quantifying plans by budgeting

(A). being aware of opportunities: This in the light of

(I) Competition

(ii) What customers want?

(iii) Our strengths

(iv) Our weakness

(B). Establishing objectives or goals:

(I). Where we want to be

(ii). what we want to accomplish

(iii) When we want to accomplish

(C). Developing primaries : It has to do with coming together to all authority concerned with the aim to obtain agreement established and circulate information and act on critical plan by using such premises as forecast is applicable to basic policies, an existing company plan. Against this background, management would be able to know in what environment internal or external the plans will operate.

(D). determining alternative cause of action: As a manager, you need to identify, what is the most promising alternative to accomplish or achieve your objectives. It is worth mentioning here that the most common problem is not finding alternative but reducing the number of alternative so that the most promising may be analyzed.

(E) Evaluating alternative cause of action: This is done by considering which alternative will give or provide the best chance of meeting the goals at their lowest, easiest and highest profit. Achieving this which maintain standard and still suit the copy long range objectives.

(F). selecting a cause: This is the real point of decision making, that is, making choice or selecting the cause of action.

(G). formulating derivative plans: This involves

(I) buying equipments

(ii) Buying materials

(iii) Hiring and training of staff

(iv) Developing new projects

(H) Quantifying plans by budgeting: The process of adding the various plan aids set important standards against which planning progress can be measured. Budget can be developed on the following

(A) Value and price sales

(B) Operating express necessary for plan

(C) Expenditure for capital equipments

However, the steps of planning entail answering the following questions.

1. Where are we now?

2. Where are we heading?

3. Do we like where we are heading?

4. If no, where should we be heading?

5. Are these destinations feasible or attractive?

6. If yes, how can we effectively get to these destinations?

7. Which type of resources do we need to achieve the desired result?

8. Which are the most efficient strategies for reaching the desired destinations?

9. What specification are needed to be determined?

10. How do we monitor our efforts?

11. What standards do we expect?

The following are problems associated with planning. These includes

1. Lack of requirement skills for planning

2. Inappropriate timing

3. Resistance to planning programmes by inside and outsiders

4. Longer time horizons staff for long range planning

5. Inadequate resources

6. Poor motivation of staff workers

7. Inflexibility of planning cost

8. Exorbitant planning cost

9. Lack of control

10. Environmental uncertainties

11. Lack of reliable and efficient data

12. Poor forecasting

The process via which planning can help the organization in setting his mission and vision

Sustaining an organization is like farming crops. Time planning is like cultivation. For an organization to achieve sustainability, the boards of directors and senior management must institutionalize a system that helps the organization to think long term as well as manages its data and day to day operations. These two tasks must be interlinked and symbolic.

The following below provides guidance and directions needed to ensure a sustainable organization

(1). Organization identity

(2). Long range strategic plan

(3). Annual operational plan

(4). Finance and other administration

(5). Long range fund raising plan

(6). Board development plan

(7). Staff development and organizational culture.